# MONEY ROCK$

## STEWARD YOUR MONEY GOD'S WAY

By Jeffrey Tan
Illustrated by Brett Cardwell

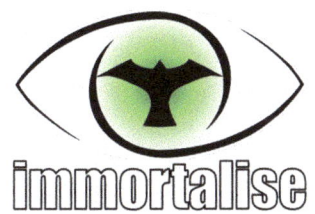

Money Rocks © copyright Jeffrey Tan 2020

Email: realgrowth@jtancoaching.com.au

No part of this publication may be reproduced, stored in a retrieval system, or transmitted in any way or by any means, electronically, mechanical, photocopying, recording or otherwise, without prior permission from author.

Requests for information should be addressed to:
www.jtancoaching.com.au

Published in Australia by Immortalise

ISBN    paperback  978-0-6488957-1-8
              ebook  978-0-6488957-2-5

Scripture taken from

THE HOLY BIBLE,

CONTEMPORARY ENGLISH VERSION (CEV)

Copyright © 1995 by American Bible Society.

All rights reserved

THE HOLY BIBLE,

NEW INTERNATIONAL READER'S VERSION

Copyright© 1996, 1998 International Bible Society.

Used by permission.

# FOREWORD

Jesus talked a lot about money, but unfortunately we don't!

In a world that is screaming for our kids' attention and their money, it is so important that we help our children understand the importance of how we view and handle our finances.

My desire is to see children grow up to love God and not money. In a selfish world where children are taught that it is all about them, we want to see children being givers and not takers. If we can teach these principles to children when they are young, they can grow to be responsible stewards of what God entrusts to them.

I want to see children have an eternal perspective and be storing treasures in heaven rather than here on Earth.

Matthew 6:19-20
"Don't store up treasures on Earth! Moths and rust can destroy them, and thieves can break in and steal them. Instead, store up treasures in Heaven, where moths and rust cannot destroy them, and thieves cannot break in and steal them."

This book teaches financial principles to children in a way that is biblical, relevant and practical.

I highly recommend this resource to you and pray that as your child reads this book and applies these principles in their lives, they will become fruitful disciples in God's Kingdom.

Pastor Andrew Shephard
**Edge Kidz – Pastor**
Edge Church International

# TABLE OF CONTENTS

WELCOME LETTER
CHAPTER 1 – OWNERSHIP
CHAPTER 2 – STEWARDSHIP
CHAPTER 3 – WORK
CHAPTER 4 – WANTS OR NEEDS
CHAPTER 5 – SOW GENEROUSLY
CHAPTER 6 – SAVE REGULARLY
CHAPTER 7 – SPEND WISELY
CHAPTER 8 – STAY OUT OF DEBT
CHAPTER 9 – HONESTY
CHAPTER 10 – LET'S ROCK THE WORLD
RESOURCE

Dedicated with love to:

My wife, Linda, who has been a great source of encouragement and my soul partner.
My girls, Sarah-Ann and Esther-Ann. They bring us great joy and I consider them blessings from God.
My parents, who demonstrated to me what it means to live life with contentment.

MEET THE KIDS

ANN AGE 9   SUE AGE 11   FRED AGE 13

Dear Parents,

Survey results from Indianna State University showed that:

> Young adults between 20 and 24 represent the fastest growing segment of bankruptcy filings.

> 71% of teens reported learning about money management from parents ... but only 26% of parents (of children 5-26) reported feeling prepared to teach their kids about basic personal finances.

I am so glad you have given me the opportunity to impart God's financial principles to your child.

As they embark on this exciting study guide of *Money Rocks*, your child will understand stewardship responsibilities and look at how to manage and multiply God's money His way.

This book revolves around the lives of Fred, Sue, Anne and your child. In each chapter, children will be searching biblical truths, solving questions and providing practical solutions to life's everyday challenges.

You play an important role in what your child learns. Your involvement is highly recommended for all ten chapters, as most activities can be a family fun time.

I honestly believe by sowing biblical principles to our children today, we are going to reap generations of God-fearing stewards who will influence and impact the world for Jesus tomorrow. Get ready, parents, your child is going to rock the world for Jesus.

Thank you for this partnership.

Sincerely,
Jeffrey Tan.

# Chapter ONE
# OWNERSHIP

Sue took her favourite bear away from her sister.

"HEY!! THIS IS MY BEAR! I BOUGHT IT WITH MY OWN MONEY. I AM THE BOSS OF IT. SO GIVE IT BACK TO ME!"

Does Sue really own the toy bear?

_____

## WHAT THE WORD SAYS...

1 Chronicles 29:11 *"...Everything in heaven and on earth belongs to you (Lord)..." (NIRV)*

1 Chronicles 29:14 *"...Everything comes from you. We've given back to you only what comes from you" (NIRV)*

## Chapter ONE – OWNERSHIP

1 Corinthians 10:26
"The earth and everything in it belong to the Lord."  (CEV)

Psalm 50:10
"Every animal in the forest already belongs to me.
And so do the cattle on a thousand hills." (NIRV)

What does GOD own?

_____

Psalm 24:1 "The earth and everything on it
belong to the LORD.
The world and its people belong to him." (CEV)

# Chapter ONE – OWNERSHIP

"SINCE GOD OWNS EVERYTHING THAT I HAVE, THE RIGHT THING I SHOULD DO IS TO _ _ _ _ _ _ MY TOY BEAR WITH MY SISTER,"

said Sue.

## ACTIVITY TIME...

## GOD IS THE ULTIMATE OWNER

Start reading Genesis chapter 1.

WHOAH! WHO MADE THIS AWESOME UNIVERSE?

_ _ _

Name something that God created that you think is absolutely AMAZING !!! And why?

_ _ _ _ _ _ _ _ _ _ _ _ _
_ _ _ _ _ _ _ _ _ _ _ _ _
_ _ _ _ _ _ _ _ _ _ _ _ _ _ _ _ _ _ _ _ _ _ _ _ _ _ _ _ _ _ .

"HOW MANY DAYS DID GOD TAKE TO COMPLETE CREATION?" _

## Chapter ONE – OWNERSHIP

DO YOU KNOW THE WORLD WAS CREATED BY GOD'S SPOKEN WORDS? THERE IS POWER IN GOD'S WORDS.

Write down what God said in the order of creation (Genesis Chapter 1)

Day 1: _____

Day 2: _____

Day 3: _____

Day 4: _____

Day 5: _____

Day 6: _____

Day 7: _____

## Chapter ONE – OWNERSHIP

MEMORY VERSE...

"THE EARTH AND EVERYTHING ON IT BELONG TO THE LORD. THE WORLD AND ITS PEOPLE BELONG TO HIM."
PSALM 24:1 (CEV)

# Chapter TWO
# STEWARDSHIP

"IF GOD OWNS EVERYTHING WE HAVE, DOES THAT MEAN WE HAVE TO BE RESPONSIBLE AND TAKE GOOD CARE OF GOD'S PROPERTY?"

What does *responsibility* mean?

_____

_____

 **WHAT THE WORD SAYS...**

1 Corinthians 4:2 *"It is required in stewards that a man be found faithful."*

A "steward" is one who takes care of someone else's things. As God's stewards, we have to take good care of His things. Although we do not own God's property, we are expected to be responsible and take good care of God's property.

# Chapter TWO – STEWARDSHIP

"WHO DID GOD APPOINT AS STEWARD IN THE BEGINNING OF CREATION?"

_ _ _ _

"The Lord God took the man and put him in the Garden of Eden to _____ it and take _____ of it."
Gen 2:15 (CEV)

# Chapter TWO – STEWARDSHIP

## ACTIVITY TIME...

Do you know we have to be good stewards of God's animals and nature?

There was a family whom God appointed to take care of many animals during a prolonged flood from the Bible. Do you know who?

------------------------------

Do you think it was easy to look after all of those animals in the ark? (TICK a box)
- ☐ EASY
- ☐ O.K.
- ☐ A LITTLE HARD
- ☐ HARD
- ☐ VERY HARD

Can you think of some duties and responsibilities the family had to do while they were in the ark?

_____
_____
_____
_____
_____

# Chapter TWO – STEWARDSHIP

DO YOU KNOW WE ARE TO BE GOOD STEWARDS AT HOME AND SCHOOL?

Name 3 things we can do to become good stewards at home.

1. _____
2. _____
3. _____

Do you know we are to be good stewards of God's money and time?

 **WHAT THE WORD SAYS...**

(Read Mat 25:14-30)

Jesus told us a parable of a man going on a long journey who entrusted his property and possessions to three servants.

When the owner returned, he called all the servants to report what they did with their money.

The first and second servant multiplied their talents. The owner was pleased with them because they were faithful in growing the money for him.

## Chapter TWO – STEWARDSHIP

In return the owner rewarded them with more responsibilities.

The third servant came back with zero growth.

Our stewardship responsibility is to faithfully multiply and manage God's resources well.

As God's stewards, we have to answer to God one day for all our actions.

Which response would you like to hear from God when you meet Him one day?

_____

_____

GREAT! BE ENCOURAGED BECAUSE GOD HAS CHOSEN YOU AND HAS GREAT THINGS PLANNED!

# Chapter TWO – STEWARDSHIP

MEMORY VERSE...

"...OUR FIRST DUTY IS TO BE FAITHFUL TO THE ONE WE WORK FOR."
1 CORINTHIANS 4:2 (CEV)

"You have done well, good and faithful servant! You have been faithful with a few things. I will put you in charge of many things. Come and share your master's happiness!"
Matthew 25:21 (NIRV)

## Chapter THREE
## WORK

WHAT THE WORD SAYS...

Genesis 2:15 *"The Lord God took man and put him in the Garden of Eden to work it and take care of it."* (CEV)

**God gave Adam work responsibilities right from the beginning of creation.**

Proverbs 6:10-11 *"Sleep a little. Doze a little. Fold your hands and twiddle your thumbs. Suddenly, everything is gone, as though it had been taken by an armed robber."* (CEV)

## Chapter THREE - WORK

Ecclesiastes 9:10 *"Work hard at whatever you do..."* (CEV)

Colossians 3:23 *"Work at everything you do with all your heart. Work as if you were working for the Lord, not for human masters."* (NIRV)

2 Thes 3:10 *"If you don't work, you don't eat."* (CEV)

Since Fred has no money, what will he need to do if he wants to buy an ipod?

_____

> "IS GOING TO SCHOOL AND STUDYING CONSIDERED AS WORK?" ASKED SUE.

What do you think and why?

_____
_____

What should my attitude be towards school, doing my homework or house chores?

_____
_____

## Chapter THREE – WORK

## ACTIVITY TIME...

"WORK IS HARD AND BORING,
AND I AM TOO YOUNG TO WORK,"

said Fred.

King David was the youngest in his family and his father sent him to look after sheep as a young boy. He had to feed them, clean them and watch the sheep so that none of them got lost.

Would you consider that as hard work?

_____

What work can Fred do at home?
Can you name 5 house chores?

1. _____
2. _____
3. _____
4. _____
5. _____

# Chapter THREE – WORK

1. DRAW a face to show how Fred is feeling.

2. Place a TICK in the circle for a good attitude towards work ✓

...Or a CROSS in the circle for the wrong attitude towards work. ✗

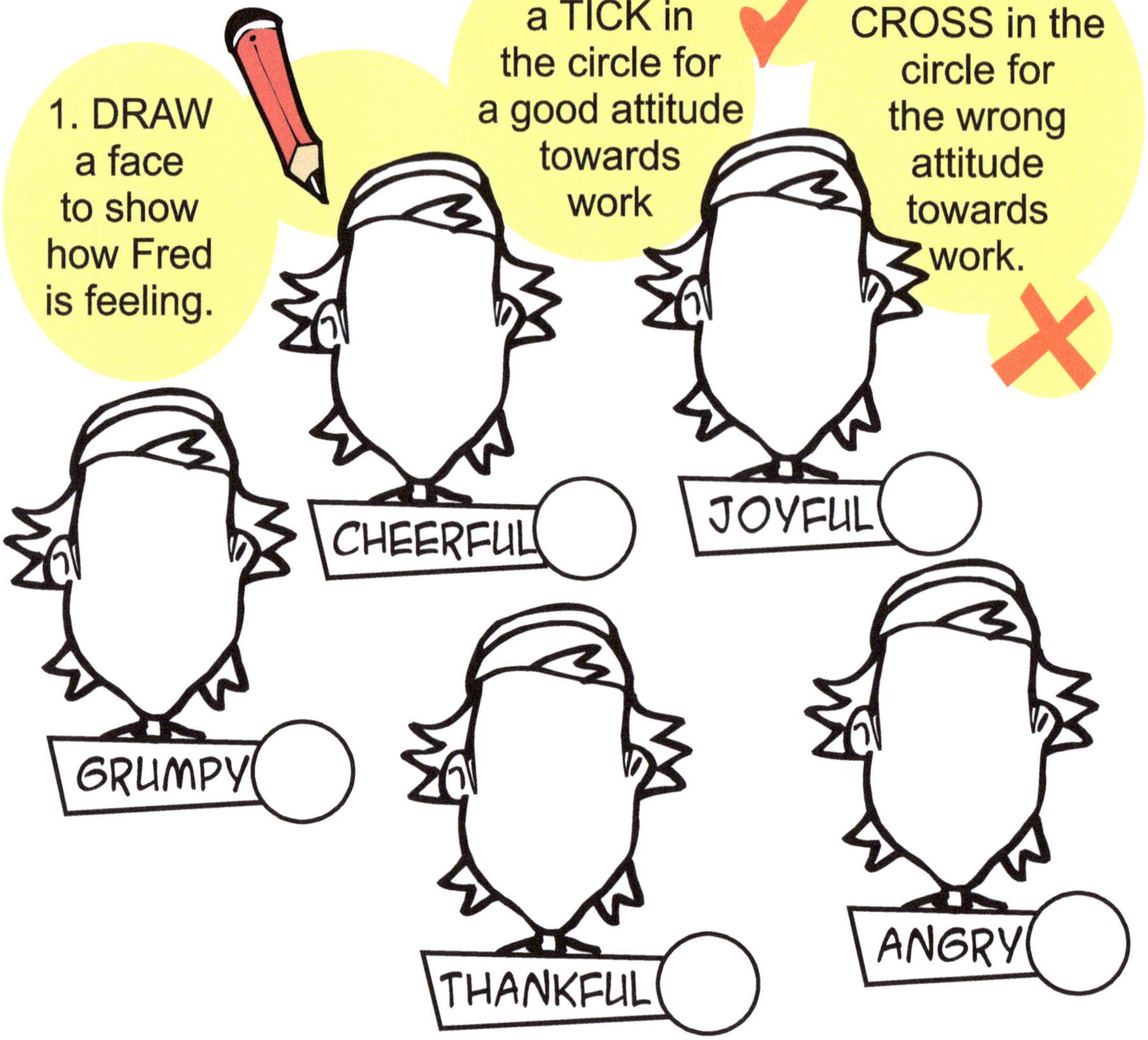

CHEERFUL ○

JOYFUL ○

GRUMPY ○

THANKFUL ○

ANGRY ○

Instead of expecting pocket money from our parents, what can we do to earn pocket money?

------------------------------------------------
------------------------------------------------

## Chapter THREE – WORK

MEMORY VERSE...

" WHATEVER YOU DO, DO YOUR WORK HEARTILY AS FOR THE LORD. "
COLOSSIANS 3:23

I BETTER ASK DAD IF HE NEEDS A HAND ...

# Chapter FOUR
# WANTS OR NEEDS

"WOW, IF I HAVE MONEY, I'M GONNA BUY MYSELF THE LATEST IPOD AND WII. MY FRIENDS HAVE THEM AND I THINK IT'S REALLY COOL TO HAVE THEM TOO!"

"IF I GET MONEY, I WANT TO BUY A NINTENDO DS AND A MOBILE PHONE!"

**WHAT THE WORD SAYS...**

Psalm 24:1 *"The earth and everything on it belong to the LORD. The world and its people belong to him."* (CEV)

1 Timothy 6:6-7 "You gain a lot when you live a godly life. But you must be happy with what you have. We did not bring anything into the world. We can't take anything out of it." (NIRV)

# Chapter FOUR – WANTS OR NEEDS

Remember that we own nothing and everything we have comes from God and belongs to Him.

We are stewards and managers of God's resources.

Does God want us to spend His money on everything we want or desire? What do you think?

------------------------------------------------

------------------------------------------------

Bad spending habits involves buying things that we **do not really NEED** or we take very little time to think through before making the purchase.

HOW DO YOU KNOW WHAT IS A 'NEED' OR A 'WANT'?

# Chapter FOUR – WANTS OR NEEDS

Before you decide if you should buy something, ask these simple questions:

A. Is it possible to live without it?

B. Is it possible to delay the purchase?

If you answered 'Yes' to both questions, it is very likely a 'Want'. You don't really need it, but you want it.

You should try to limit your buying to things you really need before you start buying the things you want. As God's managers, we must not mess up the little money that we have.

What will God think if we have bad spending habits and make poor buying choices?

---

## ACTIVITY TIME...

Can you choose which items you would consider as Needs and Wants?

| Choices | Needs | Wants |
|---|---|---|
| Mobile Phone | | |
| Gaming Console | | |
| Branded Jeans | | |
| Jogging shoes | | |
| Non branded T-shirt | | |

## Chapter FOUR – WANTS OR NEEDS

MEMORY VERSE...

" YOU GAIN A LOT WHEN YOU LIVE A GODLY LIFE, BUT YOU MUST BE HAPPY WITH WHAT YOU HAVE. "
1 TIMOTHY 6:6 (NIRV)

## Chapter FIVE
# SOWING GENEROUSLY

I WORKED REAL HARD THIS WEEK. I HELPED TO WASH MY DAD'S CAR AND MOWED THE LAWN. DAD GAVE ME $10 FOR ALL THE WORK I DID !!!

I HELPED TO MOP ALL THE FLOORS. MUM PAID ME $5 !!

I DIDN'T DO AS MUCH WORK AS I SHOULD'VE OVER THE WEEKEND. I EARNED $1 FOR TAKING THE TRASH OUT!

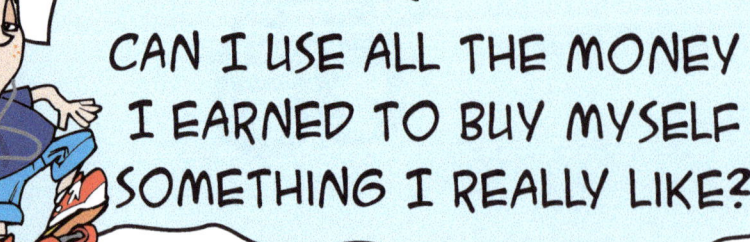

CAN I USE ALL THE MONEY I EARNED TO BUY MYSELF SOMETHING I REALLY LIKE?

## Chapter FIVE – SOWING GENEROUSLY

## WHAT THE WORD SAYS…

Leviticus 27:30
*"Ten percent of everything you harvest is holy and belongs to me, whether it grows in your fields or on your fruit trees." (CEV)*

Malachi 3:10
*'Bring the entire tenth to the storerooms in my temple. Then there will be plenty of food. Put me to the test,' says the Lord. (NIRV)*

2 Corinthians 9:6-7
*"Here is something to remember. The one who plants only a little will gather only a little. And the one who plants a lot will gather a lot. You should each give what you have decided in your heart to give. You shouldn't give if you don't want to. You shouldn't give because you are forced to. God loves a cheerful giver." (NIRV)*

Matthew 19:21
*"If you want to be perfect, go, sell your possessions and give to the poor, and you will have treasure in heaven." (NIRV)*

Acts 20:35
*"It is more blessed to give than to receive." (NIRV)*

# Chapter FIVE – SOWING GENEROUSLY

## Sowing Principles:

Fill in the blanks with the words below:

CHEERFUL        POOR        TEN
AFTER        GOD        FREE OFFERINGS

### PRINCIPLE # 1:
The first thing we need to do is to tithe _____ %
of our income or pocket money.
This is a proportion of what we earned.

### PRINCIPLE # 2:
Our tithe should be given to _____. (Discuss how)

### PRINCIPLE # 3:
God wants us to give with a _____
heart at all times.

I can be cheerful about giving because God has blessed me
and He has enabled me to bless others.

### PRINCIPLE # 4:
God wants us to help the _____ and needy people.

### PRINCIPLE # 5:
Whatever amount you give after tithes is called _____.

## Chapter FIVE – SOWING GENEROUSLY

# ACTIVITY TIME...

How many 10 cent coins make $1? _____

 x _____ = $1

How many 10 cent coins make $2? _____

One-Tenth can be written as $\frac{1}{10}$

It means one out of ten equal parts.

**Colour one-tenth of the coins in red.**

## Chapter FIVE – SOWING GENEROUSLY

1 tenth of $1 is _____ cents
1 tenth of $2 is 20 cents
1 tenth of $3 is 30 cents.
1 tenth of $4 is _____ cents
1 tenth of $5 is _____ cents

How much should Fred, Sue and Ann tithe?
_____, _____ and _____

TITHE — OFFERING

**How to start sowing:**

**STEP 1:** Prepare a Sow Box (Sowing account) and label it with tithe & offering. Make a divider in the box for both of these.

**STEP 2:** Put in your tithe amount into the Sow box. (This amount belongs to God.)

**STEP 3:** Ask yourself if you know of anyone who needs financial help. If not, ask your Children's Pastor if there is a mission work you can help.

**STEP 4:** Find out how much money they need.

**STEP 5:** Ask God how much you should contribute. You can give any amount of your money towards helping the needy. (Remember to give cheerfully)

**STEP 6:** Bring the money from the Sow Box to church and put it in the offering bag.

## Chapter FIVE – SOWING GENEROUSLY

MEMORY VERSE...

"IT IS MORE BLESSED TO GIVE THAN TO RECEIVE."
ACTS 20:35 (NIRV)

## Chapter SIX
# SAVING REGULARLY

"ALRIGHT, I HAVE GIVEN MY TITHE AND AN EXTRA 10% TO HELP THE POOR. DOES THAT MEAN I CAN NOW SPEND ALL THE $8 I HAVE LEFT?"

asked Fred eagerly.

## WHAT THE WORD SAYS...

Proverbs 21:20
"Be sensible and store up precious treasures - don't waste them like a fool." (CEV)

Proverbs 22:3
"When you see trouble coming, don't be stupid and walk right into it - be smart and hide." (CEV)

Proverbs 30:25
"Ants, who seem to be feeble, but store up food all summer long" (CEV)

## Chapter SIX – SAVING REGULARLY

Genesis 41:48
*"Joseph collected all the food produced in those seven years of abundance in Egypt and stored it in the cities..." (NIRV)*

Why do ants need to store their food in summer?

------------------------------------

What happened after 7 years of good harvest when Joseph was Prime Minister of Egypt?

------------------------------------

What do you think would have happened if Joseph had not saved for famine?

------------------------------------

Do you know how much Joseph saved every year from the crops he harvested? (Read Genesis 41:34)

------------------------------------

# Chapter SIX – SAVING REGULARLY

What do you think Fred, Sue and Ann should do with their money after they have set aside for sowing?

------------------------------------

## ACTIVITY TIME...

**Prepare a Savings Box** (Savings account) and label it.

Record the date and the amount of money that was put inside the box. This will help you to keep track of the amount inside the box.

Saving what you have today will help you prepare for the times ahead.

### How much money should you save?
You need to decide on an amount.

It can be a fixed amount or a fixed percentage just like tithing.

# Chapter SIX – SAVING REGULARLY

> I WANT TO SAVE _____ EVERY WEEK
> OR _____% OF MY MONEY
> EARNED EVERY WEEK.

Once you have decided,
put that amount into the Savings Box.

Ask your parents to start a savings account for you at your local bank.

Transfer the money from your Savings Box to your savings account.

Your bank will pay you an interest because you just lent your money to the bank.

Chapter SIX – SAVING REGULARLY

MEMORY VERSE...

" ANTS, WHO SEEM TO BE FEEBLE, BUT STORE UP FOOD ALL SUMMER LONG."
PROVERBS 30:25 (CEV)

## Chapter SEVEN
# SPENDING WISELY

"I SAW THE LATEST AND COOLEST TOY PUPPY ON TV. IT CAN OBEY SIMPLE INSTRUCTIONS AND THEY LOOKED SO-OOO CUTE! I WANT TO BUY IT BUT I DON'T HAVE ENOUGH MONEY!"

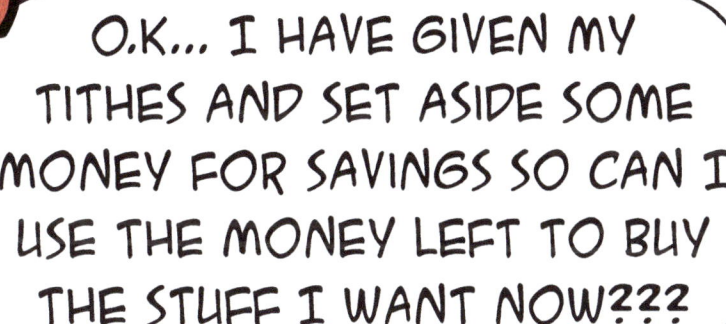

"O.K... I HAVE GIVEN MY TITHES AND SET ASIDE SOME MONEY FOR SAVINGS SO CAN I USE THE MONEY LEFT TO BUY THE STUFF I WANT NOW???"

## WHAT THE WORD SAYS...

Philippians 4:11
*"I am not complaining about having too little. I have learned to be satisfied with whatever I have."*

# Chapter SEVEN – SPENDING WISELY

1 Tim 6:6
*"But you must be happy with what you have."* (NIRV)

Heb 13:5
*"Don't fall in love with money. Be satisfied with what you have. The Lord has promised that he will not leave us or desert us."* (CEV)

God wants us to be content and thankful with what we already have.

There are many things we want in life, but it is impossible to own everything.

It is alright to buy new things for yourselves, but you need to be selective.

# Chapter SEVEN – SPENDING WISELY

**What do you think Sue can do?**

FIRST: Find out how much the toy puppy will cost.

SECOND: Count how much money she has.

THIRD: Start saving her money for the toy puppy

# ACTIVITY TIME...

Prepare a Spending Box or Jar and label it.

Put all your money you want to spend in the Spending Box.

Record the date and the amount of money that was put inside the box.

This will help you to keep track of the amount inside the box.

# Chapter SEVEN – SPENDING WISELY

Should Fred spend all the money from the Spending Box? \_\_\_ Why? _____

What are the 2 simple questions you should ask yourself before you decide to buy? (See chapter 4)

A. Is it possible to live _____ it?

B. Is it possible to _____ the purchase?

List three things you want to buy and write how much each item costs:

1ST CHOICE _____ $ _____
2ND CHOICE _____ $ _____
3RD CHOICE _____ $ _____

**IF I EARNED $6 THIS WEEK FROM DOING HOUSE CHORES, HOW MUCH SHOULD I TITHE?**

_____

How much will YOU put into each box?

SOW: _____

SAVE: _____

SPEND: _____

## Chapter SEVEN – SPENDING WISELY

MEMORY VERSE...

"I AM NOT COMPLAINING ABOUT TOO LITTLE. I HAVE LEARNED TO BE SATISFIED WITH WHATEVER I HAVE."
PHILIPPIANS 4:11 (CEV)

## Chapter EIGHT
# STAY OUT OF DEBT

"I DON'T HAVE MUCH MONEY TO SPEND. CAN I BORROW MONEY FROM FRED TO BUY MY FAVOURITE TOY?"

**'Debt'** is when you owe somebody a sum of money.

## WHAT THE WORD SAYS...

Romans 13:8
*"Pay everything you owe..."* (NIRV)

Proverbs 22:7
*"Rich people rule over those who are poor. Borrowers are slaves to lenders"* (NIRV)

# Chapter EIGHT – STAY OUT OF DEBT

Do you think Ann should borrow money from Fred? _____

According to Proverbs, when someone borrows money, the borrower becomes a _____ to the lender.

## ACTIVITY TIME...

What do you think Ann could do? List 3 things.

1. _____
2. _____
3. _____

## MEMORY VERSE...

"KEEP OUT OF DEBT
AND OWE NO MAN ANYTHING!"
ROMANS 13:8

# Chapter NINE
# BEING HONEST

"CHECK OUT THIS WALLET I FOUND! THERE'S A $50 NOTE AND A FEW PLASTIC CARDS... LIKE A DRIVER'S LICENCE AND STUFF ... BUT CAN I KEEP THE MONEY INSIDE?"

## WHAT THE WORD SAYS...

Leviticus 19:11
"'Do not steal. Do not tell lies.
Do not cheat one another" (NIRV)

Ephesians 4:25
"So each of you must get rid of your lying. Speak the truth to your neighbour.
We are all parts of one body." (NIRV)

## Chapter NINE - BEING HONEST

What do you think Sue should do?

Tick which one you think is right.

A. Take the money and spend it.
B. Take the money and give it to Ann because she needs it.
C. Bring the wallet to the nearest police station so that the owner can be contacted.

> God is looking for good and faithful stewards at all times. (Matthew 25:21 and 23)

What do you think are some good qualities of a steward that God will be looking for? Name three:

1. _____
2. _____
3. _____

## Chapter NINE – BEING HONEST

MEMORY VERSE...

"DO NOT STEAL.
DO NOT TELL LIES.
DO NOT CHEAT ONE ANOTHER."
LEVITICUS 19:11 (NIRV)

# Chapter TEN
# ROCK THE WORLD for JESUS

"WELCOME TO ROCK THE WORLD FOR JESUS CONFERENCE. EVERYONE HERE TONIGHT CAN BE PART OF GOD'S BIG PLAN TO CHANGE THE WORLD!"

said Pastor Phil as thousands of children and parents cheered and clapped.

"I THINK IT'S AWESOME TO BE PART OF GOD'S PLAN TO CHANGE THE WORLD FOR HIM!"

"I'M SO-OO GLAD I CAN DO ALL THINGS THROUGH JESUS..."

"I REALLY WANT TO KNOW HOW I CAN ROCK THE WORLD FOR JESUS!"

The cheering and clapping got louder.

## Chapter TEN – "ROCK THE WORLD FOR JESUS"

### Did you know?

**A child dies every three seconds as a result of extreme poverty. More than 1 billion people around the world live in abject (without hope) poverty on less than $1 a day. About 800 million people go to bed hungry every night and more than 6000 people die from HIV/AIDS every day.**
(Source: makepovertyhistory.com.au)

In other words, approximately 25,000 children die as a result of extreme poverty every day.

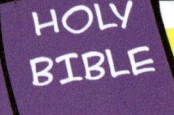

## WHAT THE WORD SAYS...
### about helping the poor?

Proverbs 3:27
"Do all you can for everyone who deserves your help." (CEV)

Proverbs 19:17
"Caring for the poor is lending to the Lord, and you will be well repaid." (CEV)

Proverbs 28:27
"Giving to poor will keep you from poverty, but if you close your eyes to their needs, everyone will curse you." (CEV)

Luke 10:27
"The scriptures say,
Love the Lord your God with all heart, soul, strength, and mind.
They also say, to Love your neighbour as much as you love yourself." (CEV)

# Chapter TEN – "ROCK THE WORLD FOR JESUS"

"TO LOVE GOD AND TO LOVE OUR NEIGHBOUR IS A COMMANDMENT AND NOT A CHOICE," said Pastor Phil.

John 13:34-35
"But I am giving you a new command. You must love each other, just as I have loved you. If you love each other, everyone will know that you are my disciples." (CEV)

WHO ARE MY NEIGHBOURS? asked Sue silently.

Jesus explained this very clearly using **'The Good Samaritan'** parable. (Luke 10:30-37).

# Chapter TEN – "ROCK THE WORLD FOR JESUS"

Jesus ended the parable by asking a question.
"Which one of these three people was a real neighbour to the man who was beaten up by robbers?"

Do you think God was only referring to people who live next door to your home?
WRITE WHO YOU THINK YOUR NEIGHBOURS ARE : _____
_____
_____,

Jesus expects us to be neighbours to anyone who is in need whenever we can.

God loves everyone and He does not want His children to live in extreme poverty. God has chosen us to be part of His plan to help those in needs.

## LET'S ROCK THE WORLD TOGETHER

When you use your money to help the poor, you help turn lives around.

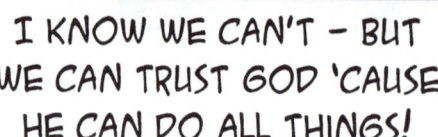

BUT I'M ONLY A KID WITH HARDLY ANY MONEY. I CAN'T DO ALL OF THIS. IT'S JUST NO WAY !!!

I KNOW WE CAN'T – BUT WE CAN TRUST GOD 'CAUSE HE CAN DO ALL THINGS!

# Chapter TEN – "ROCK THE WORLD FOR JESUS"

## '5 loaves and 2 small fish' Principle (John 6:5-13)

"There is a boy here who has five
small loaves of barley bread and two fish.
But what good is that with all these people?"

Jesus saw a large crowd of people who were tired and hungry and He asked His disciples to show hospitality to them. Jesus was not looking at how much money the disciples had because He already knew they didn't have enough to feed 5000 people.

He was looking for generous givers who were willing to give whatever they can so that His blessings and miracles can flow through them.

One boy's obedience and generosity opened the window of heaven that blessed 5000 people.

He really rocked the world for Jesus.

# Chapter TEN – "ROCK THE WORLD FOR JESUS"

## ACTIVITY TIME...

Proverbs 19:17
*"Caring for the poor is lending to the Lord, and you will be well repaid."* (CEV)

How did God repay the boy for giving his dinner away?

_____

Fred, Sue and Ann heard that many children in Cambodia do not attend school because their parents are very poor.

They found out that it only cost $200 a year to sponsor a child to school. Their local church is running this program. They have a combined savings of $30.

They really want to help sponsor a child but they are short of $170. Can you help them so that they can Rock The World for Jesus?

Below are a few suggestions they have come up with.

1. Just give the $30 to the church
2. Ask their parents to donate $170
3. Do more house chores and earn extra money.
4. _____
5. _____
6. _____
7. _____

# WHAT OTHERS ARE SAYING ABOUT "MONEY ROCKS"

*I am grateful for such a clear and easy to understand Biblical pattern that helps kids learn the value of money from God's point of view. This is a much needed resource that will encourage kids as they begin the journey of financial stewardship.*

Ps Danny Guglielmucci (South Australia)
Senior Minister Edge Church International

*Scripturally based, simple and easy to understand, Jeffrey's book should be in the hands of every parent and teacher. If you have a passion for teaching kids that their faith applies to all of life, then you will find this a very useful tool.*

N. Lee Avery (South Australia)
Principal - Sunrise Christian School

*As a father of three girls, I have found "Money Rocks" to be a great tool to teach basic stewardship biblical patterns to my young girls.*
*It has provided us with a format that is easy to use and that has been enjoyable for my kids, as we discuss and open up the Word of God together, through Money Rocks.*

Jonathon Tumes
Financial Stewardship Manager - Edge Church International

*This book is tremendous Kingdom tool to help parents instill biblical principles into with children with regards to the topic of personal finances. It is a subject rarely taught in schools and Sunday schools and hence, without this, our children end up getting their financial values from their friends and media.*
*The Bible tells us to bring up our children in the way that they should go, so that when they are older, they will not depart from these ways. Aimed at 9-13 year olds, this is the perfect time to train our kids to handle their money in a way which honours God.*

Timothy Wong (Singapore)
Head of Research - Regional Stockbroking firm

*A great resource for Parents, Teachers and Youth Ministries*
*"Money Rocks" will help our younger generation understand God's biblical principles of money and stewardship*

Stefan Horvath,
Director Business and Finance, Full Gospel Business Australia

# THIS CERTIFICATE IS AWARDED TO

_____

## for completing MONEY ROCKS series #1

You can "Rock the World for Jesus"

Signed: _____   Date: _____

Lightning Source UK Ltd.
Milton Keynes UK
UKHW051311031020
370941UK00002BA/39